W9-ANQ-359

The Church Is a *Who*
(for ages 5-8)

by
Bernice Hogan

Illustrated by John Steiger

CBP Press
St. Louis, Missouri

Fourth Printing 1986

© 1979 by The Bethany Press
All rights reserved. No part of this book may be reproduced by any method without the publisher's written permission. Address: The Bethany Press, Box 179, St. Louis, MO 63166.

Library of Congress Cataloging in Publication Data

Hogan, Bernice.
  The church is a who.

  SUMMARY: Characterizes the church as people, not buildings.
  1. Church—Juvenile literature.   1. Church
I. Steiger, John, 1923-   II. Title.
BV600.2.H576   261.8   78-24087
ISBN O-8272-0442-6

Distributed in Canada by The G. R. Welch Company, Ltd., Toronto, Ontario, Canada.
Printed in the United States of America.

To the people of
First Christian Church,
Kearney, Nebraska,
because they have learned
to love and care.

This book is designed so that children may add their own color to the pages if they wish.

The CHURCH Is a *WHO*

Almost every THING you see is a WHAT:

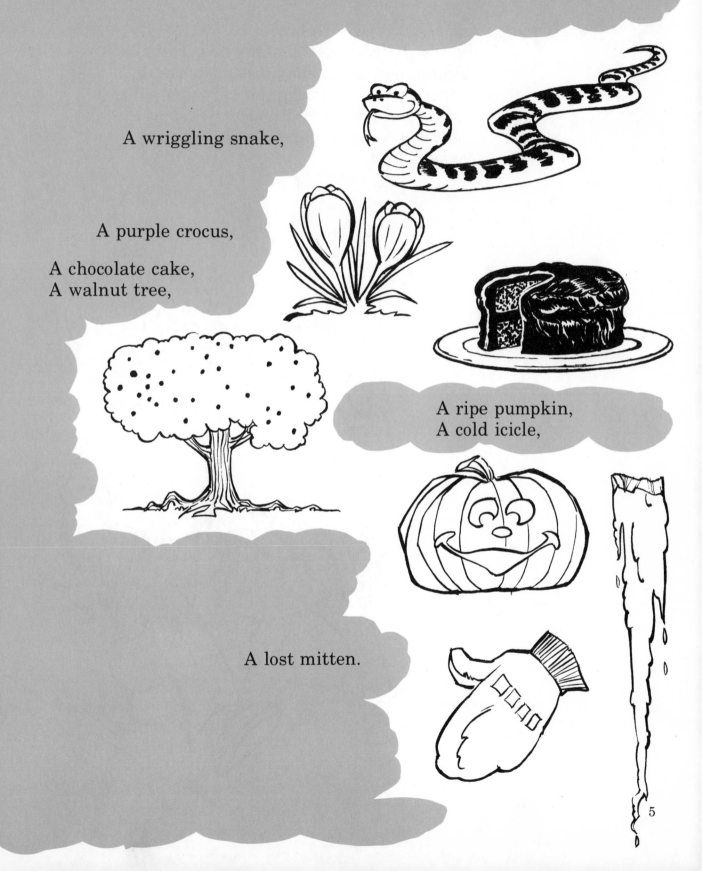

A wriggling snake,

A purple crocus,

A chocolate cake,
A walnut tree,

A ripe pumpkin,
A cold icicle,

A lost mitten.

Almost every DAY is a WHAT:
A red-heart Valentine, sending or getting,
A shining, new and happy Easter morning,
A "school-is-out" afternoon for carrying home
papers with stars, and papers with pictures,
and maybe even papers with numbers
crossed out,

A nation's birthday with flags and fried chicken
    and fireworks from the Volunteer Fire
    Department,
A "back-to-school" morning with new shoes that
    hurt and a new lunch-box that doesn't,
A Halloween evening with cats and ghosts and
    candy bars,
A Christmas moment with tree and tinsel and
    the tiny baby in the manger underneath.

Almost every PLACE you see is a WHAT:

A sunny park,
A laughing circus,
A birthday-candle party,
A splashing swimming pool,

A catsup, mustard, onion, pickle hamburger
    drive-in,
A white-frame, big-yard, day-care center,
A tall, red-brick, long-window church building.

Almost every THING you see in a church is a WHAT, too:

A gold cross,
A wooden pew,
An orange crayon,
An open Bible,
A silk bookmark,
A bent hymnal,
A scribbled picture.

A tall golfer,
A pizza server,
A doctor who's deaf,
A bus driver with freckles,
A tanned farmer,
A laughing doughnut-maker,
An airline attendant,
A typing office worker.

Every PERSON you see in a church is a WHO, too:

A youthful preacher,
A wrapped-up baby,

A smiling secretary with earrings,

A janitor with glasses,

A superintendent with brown shoes,

A teacher with things to do,

An elder with prayers.

The church IS a WHO
because it's made up of people.

It's true that churches stand in different places.

A church can be on the edge of an alfalfa field
    in Nebraska,
Or on a street corner in St. Louis.
A church can be tall when it's built in Kansas
    City,
Or it can be round in Pittsburgh, Pennsylvania.
There are churches with gold statues in Mexico,
And churches with beautiful flowers in Hawaii,
And plain, square churches in Africa or Arizona.

It's true that churches can *look* different when they have:

Stained-glass w
Tall steeples,
Palm trees outs
Brick bulletin l
Grass,
Driveways that
Gray stone wal
Thin chimneys,
Heavy brown d

vs,

s for announcements,

e,

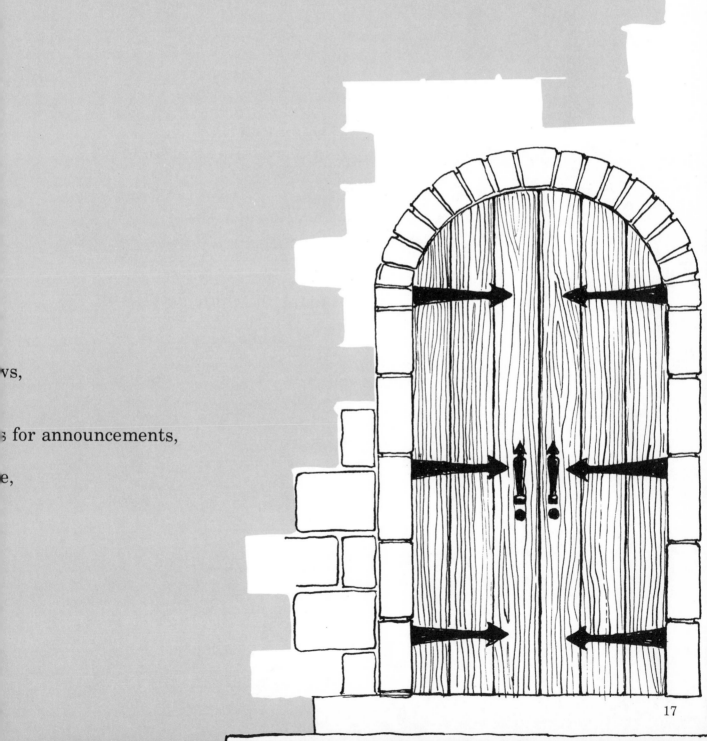

No matter how different churches look,
No matter in what different places churches stand,

Each one is a WHO
Because more important than how it looks
          or where it's built,

Are the PEOPLE both inside and outside,
For it's the PEOPLE that make the church a WHO.

You can see how the church is a WHO when people are:
    Taking roll in a church school class,
    Praying by themselves in the corner of a pew,
    Being married in the sanctuary,
    Picking up toys in the nursery,
    Teaching juniors in their classroom,
    Shaking hands with children when they come in
        the door.

The church is a WHO at many times and in many seasons:

When the Christmas manger scene is broken,
When Easter lilies stand straight,
When prayers are whispered
And sermons are not,
When a beautiful bride in white walks down the
    aisle
And when there is a funeral for an old, old person;

When everyone starts to sing the last stanza of
    a hymn
Or when someone is baptized.
When people laugh or cry,
Or when there is a celebration of an anniversary,
Or the beginning of a brand new church.

In all these times and seasons
of people and of God,
The church is best of all a WHO.

Yet the church can be people even when they're not
in a building:

When Christians go camping together,
Or calling on people new in town,
Or visiting people in nursing homes,
Or making cookies for shut-ins,
Or writing letters to moved-away people,
Or planning sunrise breakfasts,
Or traveling to retreats,
Or youth conferences,
Or just home.

Because not only is the church
    A youthful preacher,
    A wrapped-up baby,
    A smiling secretary with earrings,
    A janitor with glasses,
    A superintendent with brown shoes,
    A teacher with things to do,
    An elder with prayers. . . .

But the church is lots of other people, too:
The tall golfer,
The pizza server,
The doctor who's deaf,
The bus driver with freckles,
The tanned farmer,
The airline attendant,
The typing office worker.

The church can be PRESENT on special DAYS, too, like

A red-heart Valentine, sending or getting,

A shining new and happy Easter morning,

A "school-is-out" afternoon for carrying home
papers with stars and papers with pictures
and maybe even papers with numbers
crossed out,

A nation's birthday with flags and fried chicken
and fireworks from the Volunteer Fire
Department,

A "back-to-school" morning with new shoes that
hurt and a new lunch-box that doesn't,

A Halloween evening with cats and ghosts and
candy bars,

A Christmas moment with tree and tinsel and
the tiny baby in the manger underneath.

The church can be PRESENT at places, too, like:
    A sunny park,
    A laughing circus,
    A birthday-candle party,
    A splashing swimming pool,
    A catsup, mustard, onion, pickle hamburger
        drive-in,
    A white-frame, big-yard day-care center,
    A tall, red-brick, long-window church building.

The church can be a WHO
     whenever people need one another,
     and Jesus,
     and God;

Whenever people are glad and want to sing together,
     or talk,
     or pray;

Whenever people are sad and want to be alone
     in the sanctuary,
     or with God;

Whenever people want to share the story of Jesus
     with their friends,
     with their neighbors,
     with the people in the church kitchen,
     and the persons outside the glass windows.

That's when the church is a WHO.

For the church is never just a THING,
      never just:
             A gold cross,
             A wooden pew,
             An orange crayon,
             An open Bible,
             A silk bookmark,
             A bent hymnal,
             A scribbled picture.

The church is YOU
and ME
and all the PEOPLE of God

whenever we meet,
wherever we live,
whenever we are together.

31